TRAN**S**FORMED
O
U
L
MIND & BODY

Transformation Program Workbook

Victory Apostolic Church

20801 Matteson Avenue • Matteson, IL 60443

Rev. Andrew D. Singleton, Jr., C.P.A., M.Div. – Senior Pastor

Transformed: Soul, Mind & Body
Copyright © 2017 Victory Apostolic Church, NFP
ISBN-13: 978-1-947288-27-0
ISBN-10: 1-9472288-27-X

All rights reserved. No part of this book may be reproduced in any form without the permission of the author, except in the case of brief quotations embodied in critical articles or reviews. All Scripture quotations are taken from the Holy Bible, New International Version®, **NIV**®. Copyright © 1973, 1978, 1984, 2011 by Biblica, Inc.™ Used by permission of Zondervan. All rights reserved worldwide. www.zondervan.com.

Printed in the United States
10 9 8 7 6 5 4 3 2 1

Cover design by: Legacy Design Inc
               Legacydesigninc@gmail.com

Published by
Life To Legacy, LLC
P.O. Box 1239
Matteson, IL.
877-267-7477
www.Life2Legacy.com
Life2legacybooks@att.net

CONTENTS

Acknowledgments	5
Preface: *Building Victorious Christlike Lives*	6
Materials	10

Section 1: The Individual - Soul

Level 1: The Individual - Soul

Whole Armor of God	11
Instructions	11
Introduction	11
Importance of Wearing the Whole Armor of God	12
The Helmet of Salvation	13
The Breastplate of Righteousness	15
The Belt of Truth	17
Level One - The Soul - Measurable Outcomes	20

Level 2: The Individual - Soul

The Shield of Faith	23
The Sword of the Spirit	25
Level Two - The Soul - Measurable Outcomes	28

Level 3: The Individual - Soul

Feet Shod with the Gospel of Peace	30
The Praying Heart	33
Level Three - The Soul - Measurable Outcomes	35

Section 2: The Individual - Mind

Level 1: The Individual - Mind

Fruit of the Spirit	37
Instruction	37
Importance of Manifesting the *Fruit of the Spirit*	38

Love	39
Joy	40
Peace	42
Level 1 - The Mind - Measurable Outcomes	45

Level 2: The Individual - Mind

Patience	47
Kindness	49
Goodness	52
Level 2 - The Mind - Measurable Outcomes	54

Level 3: The Individual - Mind

Faithfulness	56
Gentleness	58
Self-Control	61
Level 3 - The Mind - Measurable Outcomes	64

Section 3: The Individual - Body

Level 1: The Individual - Body

Taking Care of Your Body	66
Introduction	67
Taking Control of What You Put in Your Body	68
Level 1 - The Body - Measurable Outcomes	71

Level 2: The Individual - Body

Taking Control of What You Do to Your Body	73
Level 2 - The Body - Measurable Outcomes	76

Level 3: The Individual - Body

Taking Control of Your Recovery Time	77
Level 3 - The Body - Measurable Outcomes	80

ACKNOWLEDGMENTS

I would like to thank everyone that played a role in putting this interactive program together (in no particular order): Pastor Andrew D. Singleton, III, Pastor Martin Stratton, Jr., Evangelist Mary Layne, Evangelist Darice Whitted, Minister Jelaine Bell, Evangelist Tracye Hutsona, Dr. Stefanie Coleman, Attorney Ronald Austin, Brother Sloan Luckie, Sister Donna Hardy, Sister Kim Garrison, and the beta group that tested the material. Without the help of these individuals, this Transformation Program workbook could not have been completed. I also want to extend a special thanks to my wife, Brenda, who during our 43 years of marriage has inspired me to be a better husband, father, and man of God.

PREFACE

From the humble beginnings of Victory Apostolic Church in 1996, Victory's foremost purpose has always been to glorify God, who created all things for His glory and honor. We are to glorify God the Father through His Son Jesus Christ, whom He has appointed heir of all things. When a believer receives Jesus Christ as their Lord and Savior, he or she becomes a new creation in Jesus Christ (2 Corinthians 5:17). From beginning to end, the Christian life is one where the believer is "being transformed" into Christ's image with ever-increasing glory (2 Corinthians 3:18). *Webster's Dictionary* defines the word "transform" as "to change in character or condition; convert." Victory's mission has always been to help transformed believers *Build Victorious Christlike Lives. Building Victorious Christlike Lives* is crucial to accomplishing the mission we all have as Christians, which is first assuring our own transformation and then helping to assure the transformation of our families and eventually transforming our surrounding communities. Jesus gave this mission to the disciples in the form of The Great Commission (Matthew 28:19-20) with a direct focus on making other disciples.

One thing that is not overtly expressed, but is implied in the mission, is that the mission is not just an external or outward responsibility. The actual mission starts internally with each of us taking responsibility for developing and maturing in Christ, so we can accomplish the mission to reach and bring others to Christ. We all have a personal mission to accomplish as our own unique individual assignment, but ultimately fulfilling the mission *of Building Victorious Christlike Lives* starts with…

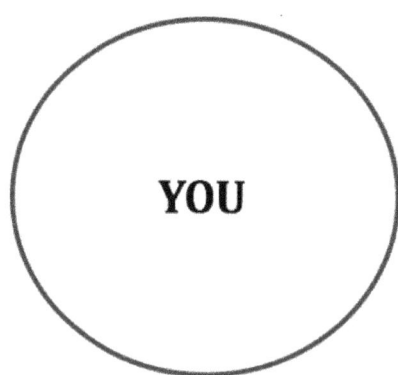

You are at the center of God's plan for the salvation of this world, and it should be an honor and a privilege to be used by God. Each of us has a role and responsibility in God's plan. That role begins with each of us stepping up to fulfill that role by first taking responsibility for our own soul, mind, and physical development as a true practicing Christian. The program you are about to embark on has been developed to help you become more effective in every aspect of your daily life. Becoming more effective begins with developing yourself from the inside out.

The Bible states, "Love the Lord your God with all your heart and with all your soul and with all your strength and with all your mind, and, love your neighbor as yourself" (Luke 10:27). In this Scripture you can see that we are being instructed to love God with our entire being or existence. We are being told this not because we are His creation and we owe this to Him, but we are being told this because this is how He first loved us; and since he first loved us, we should reciprocate.

Since God is the Creator of our souls and we are created in His Spiritual image, this means that we are all spiritual beings. The spiritual aspect of our being is the driver for all of our thoughts and actions. It is critical that every believer is born again as Jesus commanded in John 3:3-8. The soul is transformed by entering a new and holy relationship with God through the indwelling Holy Spirit. God's Spirit is Holy. The Scriptures tell us in Leviticus 20:7, "Consecrate yourselves and be holy, because I am the LORD your God." Speaking anthropomorphically, everything God thinks and does is driven by His Holiness. Holiness is the standard that we are to strive for, and holiness should be the motivation behind what we think, how we think, what we do, and how we do it.

The mind is also the means by which we are transformed into becoming more spiritual and living a life of holiness. Romans 12:2 says, "Do not conform to the pattern of this world, but be transformed by the renewing of your mind. Then you will be able to test and approve what God's will is—his good, pleasing and perfect will." The mind is not only the means by which we are transformed into living a holy life; it is also the control system for the body and controls how we act and react. The mind is the guide for our actions and reactions, and it is the place where decisions are made. Those decisions that are made will either line up with the will of God or our own will, which is the will of self. Once our minds have been transformed, then our bodies become useful instruments for carrying out God's will in this world.

The body is key for fulfilling the mission; therefore, it must be fit for the tasks that God has called us to complete. Jesus was obedient unto death and He sacrificed His life for us. All of us are not called to sacrifice our lives unto death like Jesus, but we are all called to live a transformed life that pleases God. Romans 12:1 says, "Therefore, I urge you, brothers and sisters, in view of God's mercy, to offer your bodies as a living sacrifice, holy and pleasing to God—this is your true and proper worship." It is our responsibility to Build and Live a Victorious Christlike Life, which in turn will lead others to want to do the same.

The soul is the core or the nature of the life we live. The mind is the guide that decides everything we do. The body is the instrument for carrying out the work that God has called us to do.

Human Make Up

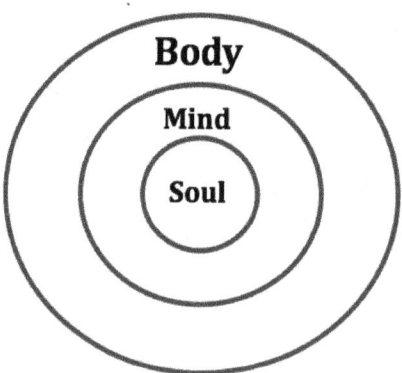

This is God's design for carrying out His purposes for each of our lives. The more we line up with His purpose, the better our lives become. Jesus states in John 10:10, "I have come that they may have life, and have it to the full." The more abundant life is given to those who find and carry out God's purpose for their lives. This is why our motto is: *Building Victorious Christlike Lives*. The Bible says that whoever is born of God overcomes the world and that the believers' faith assures victory (1 John 5:1-5).

It is the responsibility of the churches across the world to help their members build a life that finds purpose and is pleasing to God. *The Transformed Soul, Mind, and Body* program was developed to assist the members of the body of Christ, which is the Church, to fulfill their individual mission and make the Church more effective in achieving its mission too. This program is designed to assist each individual in their pursuit of *Building Victorious Christlike Lives*. The Transformational Program is set up in three parts that focus on: the individual, the family, and the community. We will first focus on the individual section in this Transformation Program workbook. The family and the community sections will be released at a later date. Since man is a three-part being in soul, mind, and body, each study of individual, family, and community transformation will encompass the soul, mind, and body triad in daily activities geared specifically towards our God-given design. God, through Jesus Christ, has given us the mission and the power to carry out the mission; but the success of the mission not only begins with YOU, it depends on YOU!

It is great to see a God-inspired vision come to actualization. I have given thought for years on how to make Victory's mission of *Building Victorious Christlike Lives* a reality in the lives of Victory's members. This transformation program has made my vision a reality.

It is my hope that this workbook will serve as a tool in transforming your spiritual life—soul, mind, and body. It is my prayer that the positive changes in your life will ultimately impact your family and community.

Congratulations on taking the next steps to continue your faithful walk with Jesus Christ and become more like Him. We are currently living in a day and age when the goal of pleasing God, instead of pleasing our flesh, is on a steady decline. This program will help you continually mature in your daily walk with Christ, and eventually you will be able to assist your family and your community in their spiritual maturation process. *The Transformed Soul, Mind, and Body* program is a great basic tool, which makes it appropriate for both genders and ages 12 and older. We hope and pray that you will take this program seriously, as this world we live in is clearly in need of some Spirit-led changes. May God be with you as you go through this spiritual experience. You are now part of our mission of *Building Victorious Christlike Lives!*

God Bless!

Senior Pastor Andrew D. Singleton, Jr. C.P.A., M.DIV
Victory Apostolic Church, Matteson, Illinois

MATERIALS NEEDED

- Bible or electronic Bible (required)

- Pen or pencil and highlighter (required)

- A device that plays music (optional)

- Smart watch/fitness tracker/app

- To track health and fitness (optional)

- Faith (required)

- An open mind and heart (required)

Section One

THE INDIVIDUAL

(THE SOUL)

WHOLE ARMOR OF GOD

INSTRUCTIONS

You are about to embark on an awesome journey, experiencing three different levels of the importance of spirituality and highlighting the importance of each piece of armor that God has called us to wear at all times. The *Whole Armor of God* consists of seven vital pieces to take on Satan in our daily life. The seven pieces that you must wear are: the Helmet of Salvation, the Breastplate of Righteousness, the Belt of Truth, the Shield of Faith, the Sword of the Spirit, Feet Shod with the Gospel of Peace, and the Praying Heart (Ephesians 6:10-18).

After reading about one of the pieces of armor, you will then answer and meditate on one question for that day ONLY, either by recording your thoughts in your personal journal or reflecting on the question throughout the day. This methodology has been devised to have you focus on one question/bullet point per day, which in turn can be used as your daily spiritual devotion. This will consist of at least **15 minutes** of daily self-reflection, Scripture reading, prayer, meditation, and worship, leading to your overall growth as a Christian. All three levels of this section focus on the soul.

The first level for the Individual Soul section consists of the Helmet of Salvation, the Breastplate of Righteousness, and the Belt of Truth. The second level for the Soul section consists of the Shield of Faith and the Sword of the Spirit. The third level for the Soul section consists of Feet Shod with the Gospel of Peace and the Praying Heart. We hope and pray you will enjoy this growth experience!

INTRODUCTION

The Apostle Paul's letter to the church of believers at Ephesus was purposely written to explain the importance and use of the *Whole Armor of God* that was needed when battling against Satan and the strongholds of spiritual darkness. There are spiritual conflicts and attacks in your life, no matter how strong in Christ you think you are.

As a believer, you must recognize the need for power and strength beyond your own human capabilities. Satan and all his evil spirits of darkness and superhuman influences are constructed to suppress and destroy the purposes of God and promote unrighteous living. Satan and all his evil spirits roam the earth mostly unhindered, seeking whom they may indwell and destroy. Their schemes can only be hindered and defeated by the power of God.

Putting on the *Whole Armor of God* will empower you to stand up and fight against the evil forces of Satan—not only in your life, but also in the lives of others (2 Corinthians 6:3-10). Paul, a Prisoner of War (POW) of spiritual warfare at the time of his writing on the subject of the Armor of God, passionately and zealously instructs us on the tactical design, purpose, and sufficiency of putting on the *Whole Armor of God*. Take this opportunity to acknowledge and consider the importance of godly defense in order to be steadfast and unmovable in every area of your life-long journey.

IMPORTANCE OF WEARING THE WHOLE ARMOR OF GOD

Today in our society, there are professing Christians that take the ideas and the sinful practices of our culture and attempt to adjust Scripture to fit their sin. In doing this, they begin to form their own made-up Christian beliefs around themselves, and NOT around the Word of God. Our culture is attempting to teach us to be tolerant of anti-biblical teaching and practices, which in turn is weakening the authority of Scripture. Putting on the *Whole Armor of God* will ground and help you to stand on God's Holy Word and His truth, which should be your ONLY standard for the truth. In spite of what our society and culture are teaching and displaying daily, being fully suited in God's Armor makes it possible for you to continue to face and overcome this dark and evil age that we live in today. Most importantly, it protects you from compromising your Christian beliefs.

LEVEL 1

(THE HELMET OF SALVATION, THE BREASTPLATE OF RIGHTEOUSNESS, AND THE BELT OF TRUTH)

The Helmet of Salvation

When a soldier prepares for a physical battle in most armies, the helmet is the last piece of armor that is put on. The helmet is vital protection against damaging or fatal blows to the head. If the head is injured, the rest of the armor will be of little use. For the believers, our helmet is Salvation. If you aren't first saved, you are of little use in the Kingdom of God. Entering spiritual battles in life without God's Armor of Salvation can also be damaging or even fatal. God requires you to be right in your living, to be right in your motives, and to be right in your mind.

God's Helmet of Salvation protects your mind against any thoughts that would cause confusion or doubt, or destroy your confidence, belief, trust, and hope in the victory over sin and death achieved by Christ (Romans 6:23). You are saved by God's grace, which is His unmerited and unearned favor on your life. This was given when Jesus gave His life for you on Calvary's Cross over 2,000 years ago. The grace of God should give you both the power and the desire to do His will.

Ask Yourself...

(Before you complete the daily "Ask Yourself" questions, read the paragraphs above and use your journal to record your answers and/or reflect throughout the day.)

Day 1: If salvation means believers are delivered and saved by grace, how do I apply salvation to my daily life? Read Ephesians 2:1-8.

Day 2: Why is it so important for me to keep God in my head and Satan out?

Day 3: How have I allowed Satan to get in my head and influence me in the past? What steps should I take to overcome his control?

Day 4: What noticeable changes have I made since God has come to live inside of me? For example, have I stopped using profanity since I put on my Helmet of Salvation?

Day 5: How important is it to protect what I allow to get into my head, such as music, movies, TV, etc.? Explain.

Day 6: Since I know the head is the area the enemy attacks the most, how willing am I to start meditating regularly to keep my head and my mind right with God daily? Read Philippians 4:8-9.

Day 7: How often do I embrace the opportunity to give God praise and thanks for my salvation and His abundant grace for not treating me as my sins deserve?

Reflection Notes

_____
_____
_____
_____
_____
_____
_____
_____
_____
_____
_____
_____
_____
_____
_____
_____
_____
_____
_____
_____
_____

The Breastplate of Righteousness

During battle, the soldier's breastplate protects the heart, lungs, and all other vital organs that sustain human life. In the heat of battle, the soldier's breastplate wards off unexpected and an overwhelming number of enemy blows. God's spiritual Breastplate of Righteousness protects your heart, and God's primary focus of transformation is in your heart. Knowledge and comprehension of God's standards of righteousness are essential defenses against unexpected and overwhelming enemy attacks and schemes. The enemy's goal is to turn you away from God's call to righteous and holy living. Righteousness is one of the fundamental divine, moral attributes of God's sovereign rule. His righteousness protects and preserves you. Righteousness is not a matter of you being morally perfect, but it is a matter of you being morally right with God (Romans 1:16-17).

Ask Yourself...

(Before you complete the daily "Ask Yourself" questions, read the paragraph above and use your journal to record your answers and/or reflect throughout the day.)

Day 8: What does it mean to live a life of righteous faith, righteous trust, and righteous belief in Christ? Read Romans 4:24-25.

Day 9: Why is it so important for my heart to be protected from Satan?

Day 10: What are some of the things that are keeping me from living righteously? For example, is it the music I listen to, TV shows I watch, the company I keep, etc.?

Day 11: What do I believe are some of the things that cause so many Christians to live unrighteous Christian lives?

Day 12: How have I recovered from bad/sinful decisions? If I haven't, what steps do I need to take to stop living my life in the past?

Day 13: How ready and willing am I to let go of known sin and take on the righteousness of God against all enemy attacks? Explain.

Day 14: Is my time in prayer, praise, worship, and the way I honor God righteous? What does my Christian walk look like outside of church?

Reflection Notes

_____
_____
_____
_____
_____

The Belt of Truth

Before a soldier would put on his armor, he would first wrap and gird his waist with a belt that held the sheath for his sword and other weapons needed for battle. That is why the belt is the first piece of armor to be mentioned—because without truth, you are lost and vulnerable to the enemy. Jesus states, "I am the way and the truth and the life. No one comes to the Father except through me. If you really know me, you will know my Father as well. From now on, you do know him and have seen him" (John 14:6-7).

The Belt of Truth is of the utmost importance in your Christian life. Without the existence of truth, there's no place to hold the believer's only offensive weapon, the Sword of the Spirit. The spiritual sword, which is the Word of God, will gird you in preparation for all spiritual warfare. The Word of God envelopes you in truth, but only if you allow it (John 17:1). Absolute truth is inseparable from the will of God in Jesus Christ. For people to trust you and for God to use you, you must be a person of integrity. His Spirit is the living, operating, and empowering force of His truth that ensures needed, continual, and effectual Christlike transformation in your life.

Ask Yourself...

(Before you complete the daily "Ask Yourself" questions, read the paragraphs above and use your journal to record your answers and/or reflect throughout the day.)

Day 15: What does it mean that Jesus is the Way, the Truth, and the Life? Read John 14:6-14.

Day 16: What benefits does being wrapped in the Belt of Truth have as it pertains to my life?

Day 17: In what ways have I not been truthful to myself in living a life that pleases God? What improvements need to be made? For example, do I lack integrity or honesty?

Day 18: What are some of the things in my life that are causing me not to live in God's truth? How can I get rid of some of the things that are hindering God's truth to be present in my life?

Day 19: What times in my life have I stood for truth? What were the benefits that came from being truthful?

Day 20: How often do I refer to the Word of God when God's truth is potentially being compromised during my free will and choice? For example, how often do I seek the Word of God when faced with the option to lie to get out of trouble?

Day 21: How often do I earnestly seek God for truth in prayer for spiritually-charged confidence, motivation, and stability? What is keeping me from seeking God's help with the stability of my life?

Reflection Notes

_____
_____
_____
_____
_____
_____
_____
_____
_____
_____
_____
_____
_____
_____
_____
_____
_____

MEASURABLE OUTCOMES FOR LEVEL 1

Individual Soul

Day 22: Have you sacrificed at least 15 minutes a day for daily devotion? This can consist of reading God's Word, meditating, seeking personal application, praying, spending silent time in God's presence, and listening in expectation for His still, quiet voice. Read Romans 12:1-2. If not, spend some time today to determine how to build in a solid 15 minutes daily for time with God.

Day 23: In which ways did you NOT allow shame, guilt, doubts, fears, and feelings to govern your thinking and dominate your actions? If you did, try sharing your battles with the Lord on a regular basis, and remember that He loves you and cares about everything that concerns you daily. Read 1Peter 1:8-9.

Day 24: Have you been able to pray daily and listen for a response from God before you finished praying? God's righteous response may sometimes take longer than we expect; however, don't move when hurried, anxious, stressed, or fearful. Wait and stand firm. Always trust in God! Read Jeremiah 32:27.

Day 25: How have you handled situations and decisions that required truth, honesty, confession, repentance, forgiveness, or an apology?

Day 26: Were you able to start a prayer journal to begin answering the questions from the individual topics.* If not, spend some time today and begin your prayer/reflection journal.

Day 27: Were you able to start a Christian blog or social media presence sharing your journey in Level 1 of the Individual Soul section? Did you try to connect with others who are on a similar journey of discovery? If not, spend some time today to begin some chatter on Level 1 of the Soul section on some type of social media platform or in a face-to-face discussion.

Day 28: What growth have you seen in your life as it pertains to the topics covered in Level 1 of the Soul section?

Day 29: What are some of the specific changes in your life that you have noticed since beginning Level 1 of the Soul section?

*All activities should include prayer and journaling for reflection purposes.

Reflection Notes

LEVEL 2

(SHIELD OF FAITH AND SWORD OF THE SPIRIT)

The Shield of Faith

The shield that was carried by the soldiers was designed specifically for defensive purposes. When raised, it was designed to block intended mortal wounds from arrows and flaming darts. It was also extremely effective in reducing the impact of advancing enemy attacks before actual hand-to-hand combat took place. Your enemy, Satan, is very crafty and he will launch a strategic attack at any time and from any angle or distance when he detects weaknesses in your life (1 Peter 5:6-9). Through the eyes of faith, you are able to withstand repeated aggressive attacks from any distance, from any position, and at all times when your Shield of Faith is active. God's armor of faith is an indispensable strategic weapon of defense, and you must utilize it daily (Hebrews 11:1-2).

Ask Yourself...

(Before you complete the daily "Ask Yourself" questions, read the paragraph above and use your journal to record your answers and/or reflect throughout the day.)

Day 30: What does it mean for me to have faith in God? Read 1 John 5:4.

Day 31: How does Satan's attacks on me affect my faith in God? Explain.

Day 32: What are some ways that I have been able to exercise my faith in God successfully in the last few weeks or months?

Day 33: When I begin to lack faith in any given situation, what do I feel are the causes?

Day 34: Do I believe that God has given me a Shield of Faith to withstand the constant attacks of Satan and the tribulations of this world? If yes, in what ways have I utilized my Shield of Faith? If not, reread "The Shield of Faith" section, 1 Peter 5:6-9, and Hebrews 11:1-2 right now.

Day 35: How often do I hesitate to make decisions based on the measure of faith God has already provided for me? How often do I have doubts about God's sufficiency? Read 2 Corinthians 5:7.

Day 36: How have I used my faith to strengthen and bless others? If I haven't, what is preventing me from sharing my faith with others? Read 1Thessalonians 3:7-8.

Reflection Notes

The Sword of the Spirit

The soldier's sword was designed especially for offensive purposes; however, it could also be raised to block aggressive blows from the enemy during close encounters. The two-edged sword was considered more dangerous than other swords used by Roman soldiers. The point of the sword was sharpened to enable it to pierce the enemy's strongest armor. When turned up, it could rip the enemy's insides to shreds. Extensive training was required to use this weapon. Your sword is the Word of God. God's written or spoken Word is strong and powerful enough to pierce and prevail against any attacks by Satan.

Reading, studying, meditating, obeying, and praying will provide you with the effectual application of God's Word to defeat the enemy and to maintain the life of righteous and holy living that is pleasing before God. There must be a personal need and desire from within—an intentional and continual press to study and obey the Word of God. The Word of God sharpens your spiritual sensitivity to God's character and awareness of His promises in order to achieve intimacy with Him. It will comfort you in times of sorrow and provide wisdom for you to better discern right from wrong according to God's truth and righteousness. Obedience to the Word of God builds competence from within when attacks of doubt and fear arise. Application of the Word of God strengthens your will to fight against contrary thoughts, attitudes, and actions that are displeasing to God (1 Corinthians 2:5). As stated, "extensive training" was required for soldiers to use their sword. Similarly, it is important for you to be taught by teachers that are biblical and teach God's truth. Taking spiritual classes are essential to your spiritual training. Our church offers multiple training classes. If your home church offers them, you must take the classes to continue your training and development in God's Word.

Ask Yourself...

(Before you complete the daily "Ask Yourself" questions, read the paragraph above and use your journal to record your answers and/or reflect throughout the day.)

Day 37: When Satan attacks, how confident am I that my Sword of the Spirit is ready and able to fight back? Explain. Read Revelation 1:16.

Day 38: How often do I allow myself to see, know, accept, and love myself as God does?

Day 39: How often do I NOT forgive myself of past sins even though God has forgiven me? How does it affect my daily life?

Day 40: Do I believe that God loved me enough to die for me? What is keeping me from loving Him back the way that He showed His love towards me?

Day 41: What does spiritual transformation mean and what are the benefits of Christians going through a spiritual transformation? How often do I attend Bible class or other spiritual training classes? Explain why or why not.

Day 42: When I'm in the presence of non-believers, in what ways have I been ashamed to disclose my belief in God's Word as my offensive weapon against sin? Read Luke 9:26.

Day 43: Can I recall a passage, circumstance, or person from the Bible that compares and validates the effective precision of God's Word in my life? Read Jeremiah 23:29.

Reflection Notes

MEASURABLE OUTCOMES FOR LEVEL 2

Individual Soul

Day 44: On a daily basis, were you able to look to the Lord first in prayer for hope and strength? Read Hebrews 12:2. If yes, what did that look like? If you weren't, spend some time today to develop a plan of action for daily interactions with God, preferably to start your day.

Day 45: Did you have a chance to start each day viewing intimacy with God as a necessity? Try to realize that it is an expression of your loving faith and your daily service unto God. Read Hebrews 11:6.

Day 46: Go back and commit to a deeper reading of the topics in Level 2 of this section.* Pick one topic that you know you still need to develop.

Day 47: Were you able to start a prayer journal to begin to answer the questions from the individual topics?* If not, begin a prayer/self-reflection journal today. If you have started the journal, how is the process going so far?

Day 48: Were you able to start a Christian blog or social media presence sharing your journey in Level 2 of the Individual Soul section? Did you try to connect with others on a similar journey of discovery? If not, spend some time today to begin some chatter on Level 2 of the Soul section on some type of social media platform or in a face-to-face discussion.

Day 49: What growth have you seen in your life as it pertains to the topics covered in Level 2 of the Soul section?

Day 50: What are some of the specific changes that you have noticed in your life since beginning Level 2 of the Soul section?

*All activities should include prayer and journaling for reflection purposes.

Reflection Notes

LEVEL 3

(FEET SHOD WITH THE GOSPEL OF PEACE
AND THE PRAYING HEART)

Feet Shod with the Gospel of Peace

In ancient warfare, foot soldiers engaged in hand-to-hand combat to take over the position of their enemies. Surefootedness and swiftness when under attack was of the utmost importance. Walking long distances was necessary since it was the primary means of transportation; therefore, footwear was specifically designed to keep the soldiers' feet protected and healthy during long marches. Small spikes or iron hobnails were driven into the soles of the shoes in order to give firm footing on uneven terrain. The soldiers needed solid footing in order to concentrate on the battle at hand.

The Gospel, the "good news" or "good tidings," is your sure footing as a Christian soldier. Embracing the Gospel assures your initiation and completion of God's divine plans and purposes in you and everyone else who loves Him as their Savior. Secured footing also commands obedience to God's righteous principles so you will not allow Satan or the feelings of inadequacy to minimize your position or callings in Christ. Your faith and trust in God's purpose, presence, and power is secure. In order for you to play a significant role in Kingdom building, you must abide in Christ. You must submit to the Father's process of spiritual transformation in order to do His will on earth as it has been ordained in heaven (Romans 12:1-2).

At all times, you must also follow the Father's instruction on giving, in accordance to His Word and with our first fruits. The believer can give of time, talent, and tithes. The "tithe" is 10 percent of your income and increases. God gave you the energy, strength, and power to earn a living so technically speaking the whole 100 percent belongs to Him. God is so awesome that even though 100 percent of your income belongs to Him, He allows you to keep 90 percent to bless you, your family, and others (Genesis 28:20-22). The 10 percent that is given to God is used by the church to be able to function in the way that God has ordained the church to function. Even though the gospel message is NOT all about money or prosperity, by all means it does take money to help spread this awesome gospel message. As God has blessed you with jobs and increases in all ways, you should show your appreciation to the faithfulness of God by tithing. Giving, in all respects, is a sign of the "mature believer's" commitment to share the Gospel of Peace.

Ask Yourself...

(Before you complete the daily "Ask Yourself" questions, read the paragraphs above and use your journal to record your answers and/or reflect throughout the day.)

Day 51: Do I believe that God has a purpose for me, even though I may not know what that purpose is yet? If yes, how does that play out in my daily living? If not, what do I feel is causing that belief of a purposeless life? Read 1 Peter 4:10.

Day 52: Are my feet and is my life grounded in God enough to withstand the attacks of the enemy? If yes, explain how? If not, explain why they aren't?

Day 53: Secured footing is a sign of obedience to God. How have I honored God in my obedience to Him?

Day 54: What ministries am I currently serving in at my church, and do they fit with my personality and the gifts that God has given me? What are some potential ministries that I can see myself involved in to help build the Kingdom of God?

Day 55: What are my thoughts on tithing, and have I been faithful to God as it pertains to giving 10 percent of my income and increases to Him? Why do I feel that tithing is important and plays a significant role in Kingdom building? If I am not tithing, what is keeping me from tithing regularly?

Day 56: Do I take the time to thank God for His peace that calms me? Do I thank God for His abiding presence that fills my heart with hope and soothes my troubled mind? Read Philippians 4:7.

Day 57: How faithful have I been when it comes to sharing the Gospel of Peace with those who have not yet come to know Christ as their Lord and Savior? How important is it for me to fulfill my call as an ambassador for the Gospel of Peace? Read Acts 1:8.

Reflection Notes

_____
_____
_____
_____
_____
_____

Reflection Notes

The Praying Heart

After all of the Armor of God is put on, it can't be energized without prayer. Since we can't do anything without God, prayer places the emphasis on God—and not the armor—for success in the believer's life. You are urged to fall on your knees in fervent prayer and worship of Him. Worship is showing reverence and adoration towards God, who is the Lover of your soul. You must attempt to worship Him daily to make sure your life stays in alignment with the Giver of Life. This position of warfare is critical and used as offense when battling the evil-doer, Satan himself. Prayer and worship will allow your heart and mind time to adjust and prepare for the reality of spiritual warfare. Prayer and worship will bring to light any wrong doing and allow you to confess your sin and turn away from it (1 John 1:18-19).

Ask Yourself...

(Before you complete the daily "Ask Yourself" questions, read the paragraph above and use your journal to record your answers and/or reflect throughout the day.)

Day 58: In what ways do I feel that prayer changes things, that God is in control, and that God is the source of my strength? Read Ephesians 6:12.

Day 59: Do I feel that I have a great prayer and worship experience with God daily? Explain. Do I feel that I should attend church every week (except for emergencies or peculiar situations) to experience God and fellowship with others?

Day 60: What are the things that are keeping me from praying and worshiping God more often when faced with difficult decisions and living for Him?

Day 61: Can I honestly say that I seek God daily in prayer and worship for His direction, or is my life too busy to have an experience with God? Explain.

Day 62: How can I use my praying heart and worship as my defense against Satan and the evils of this world?

Day 63: Am I consciously yielding to the indwelling power of the Holy Spirit, or is doing God's will still a struggle? Explain. Read Romans 8:26.

Day 64: Have I been diligent in using my time in prayer to prepare myself for God's Kingdom and my victorious Christlike transformation? Read Romans 8:29 and explain what it means.

Reflection Notes

MEASURABLE OUTCOMES FOR LEVEL 3

Individual Soul

Day 65: What time of day is best for you to be able to seek the Lord's peace, guidance, and direction in Bible reading and prayer for personal spiritual development and maturity? Why is that time of day best?

Day 66: Were you able to commit to attending/streaming Bible Study and attending Prayer Service at least one or two times per month? If not, what is keeping you from taking that step?

Day 67: Take the time today to pray for people who have hurt you in the past. Also, take the time today to pray for those people that you prefer NOT to be in their presence.

Day 68: Did you have a chance to start a Christian blog or social media presence to share your journey of Level 3 of the Individual Soul section? Did you try to connect with others on a similar journey of discovery? If not, spend some time today to begin some chatter on Level 3 of the Soul section on some type of social media platform or in a face-to-face discussion with someone.

Day 69: What growth have I seen in my life as it pertains to the topics covered in Level 3 of the Soul section?

Day 70: What are some of the specific changes that you have noticed in your life since beginning Level 3 of the Soul section?

Day 71: What overall changes have you noticed in your life after completing the Soul portion of the Individual section of this interactive program? How was it beneficial?

*All activities should include prayer and journaling for reflection purposes.

Reflection Notes

_____
_____
_____
_____
_____
_____

Section Two

THE INDIVIDUAL
(THE MIND)
FRUIT OF THE SPIRIT

INSTRUCTIONS

You are about to embark on another awesome journey, experiencing three different levels of the importance of discipline over your mind, by highlighting how the *Fruit of the Spirit* plays a vital role in your daily living for Jesus Christ. The *Fruit of the Spirit* consist of nine gifts that help your mind stay focused on Jesus. "The fruit of the Spirit is love, joy, peace, patience, kindness, goodness, faithfulness, gentleness, and self-control. Against such things there is no Law. Those who belong to Christ Jesus have crucified the flesh with its passions and desires. Since we live by the Spirit, let us keep in step with the Spirit"(Galatians 5:22-25).

Once you have read a section on each *Fruit of the Spirit*, you will then answer and meditate on one question for that day ONLY and record your thoughts in your personal journal. This part of the program is designed for you to focus on one question/bullet point per day and can be used as your daily spiritual devotion. Be prepared to spend at least **15 minutes** of daily self-reflection, Scripture reading, prayer, meditation, and worship, which should result in your overall improvement as a Christian. The first level for the Individual Mind section focuses on love, joy, and peace. The second level will consist of exploring patience, kindness, and goodness. Lastly, the third level focuses on faithfulness, gentleness, and self-control. We hope and pray you will enjoy and grow!

INTRODUCTION

As a pastor, one of my best Christmas gifts from members is boxed fruit from *Harry & David®*. The fruit is always fresh, smells good, and tastes great! The *Fruit of the Spirit* is exhibited in the believer's life through faith in Christ Jesus and submissiveness to God's will. It is an outward indicator of an inward salvation.

IMPORTANCE OF MANIFESTING THE
FRUIT OF THE SPIRIT

It is extremely important for Christians to be led by the Spirit and not by the fleshly desires of this world. When you decide to go through the spiritual transformation process, God produces the fruit that begins to grow inside of you. At times, believers do not exhibit as much of the Spirit's Fruit as we should. However, the Holy Spirit convicts you to better exhibit the Fruit in your everyday life. You serve an abundant God, which means that He intended you to also live in abundance, according to His will. Now is the time, more than ever, for you as a transformed believer to focus your daily thoughts on God. You have access to so many things through technology that can easily enter your mind and take your attention away from what God has called you to do, and you must protect your calling at all cost (Proverbs 23:7).

LEVEL 1

(LOVE, JOY, AND PEACE)

LOVE

The version of love used as a *Fruit of the Spirit* isn't the warm feelings of love we have with each other, but it is an attitude of devotion and good will. Love gives freely, even if we feel the person doesn't deserve it or is unworthy of receiving it. This feeling of love, as it pertains to the *Fruit of the Spirit*, gives without the ulterior motive of looking to get something in return. Jesus gave you the best example of love to follow in His daily interactions and lifestyle of seeking and obeying the will of His Father. He even showed this type of submissive love while being crucified for your sins. He was able to put His feelings of pain aside because of the unconditional love He has for you (Matthew 22:36-40).

Ask Yourself...

(Before you complete the daily "Ask Yourself" questions, read the paragraph above and use your journal to record your answers and/or reflect throughout the day.)

Day 72: How do I feel about God loving me so much that He sent His Son to die for my sins? Read John 3:16.

Day 73: What things or events have happened in my life that have affected my ability to love the way that God has called me to love? What are some of the steps that I need to take to move past hurt and live a loving, God-led life?

Day 74: How often am I motivated to do for others like Christ did? For example, am I always expecting something in return when I choose to show my love or give my love to others? Explain.

Day 75: How does my love for God trickle down to my love for others and myself?

Day 76: In what ways do I feel the love of God in my daily life? Explain.

Day 77: Since I know the enemy, Satan, wants to get rid of the love I have in my heart for God. What are the best ways for me to ensure he doesn't affect my love for God and others?

Day 78: How often do I embrace the opportunity to show my love for God through the way that I give of my time, talents, and money? Is this giving a direct reflection of my love for God? Explain.

Reflection Notes

_____
_____
_____
_____
_____
_____
_____
_____
_____
_____
_____
_____
_____
_____
_____

JOY

Joy and happiness are similar, but they are not synonymous. Happiness is dependent upon what happens in your daily life, whether good or bad. Joy, as it pertains to the *Fruit of the Spirit*, is totally independent from what occurs in your life. Jesus still showed joy during the worst moments of His life. This is what makes the gift of joy a spiritual and supernatural emotion from God that is needed in those moments when trials and tribulations come into your life. The gift of joy gives you the unique ability to handle life's situations that are not always positive. Without this gift, it is extremely easy for your mind to drift into non-spiritual areas when life appears to be negative. Always remember that the Joy of the Lord is your strength (Nehemiah 8:10). The Bible gives us the awesome example of women in labor to illustrate joy. A women may be in pain while in labor, but the pain is only temporary. As soon as she sees her child, her pain turns into joy (John 16:21-24). Similarly, the pain that Jesus Christ endured on Calvary's Cross was turned into joy because He knew He was fulfilling His mission of being your Savior! (See Hebrews 12:1-2.)

Ask Yourself...

(Before you complete the daily "Ask Yourself" questions, read the paragraph above and use your journal to record your answers and/or reflect throughout the day.)

Day 79: What does it mean to me that the Joy of the Lord is my strength? How can I apply this to my daily living? Read Psalm 28:7.

Day 80: What does it mean to me to know that God gave me joy and since He gave it to me that means others and this world can't take it away from me? Explain.

Day 81: When God wakes me up in the morning, do I feel joyful that He has blessed me to see another day in spite of how I feel? Explain.

Day 82: How often do I exercise my supernatural gift of joy and stay positive in negative situations? How often do I look for the negatives in situations? Explain.

Day 83: Am I experiencing a life of joy on a regular basis, or is my happiness contingent on things going smoothly? Explain.

Day 84: Why does Satan try so hard to invade my mind and attempt to take the gift of joy that God has given me?

Day 85: Joy is often mentioned during the Christmas season; why do I feel that a large emphasis of joy revolves around the birth of Jesus Christ?

Reflection Notes

_____
_____
_____
_____
_____
_____
_____
_____
_____

PEACE

    Peace as a *Fruit of the Spirit* is only given to those believers who have experienced the peace with God that comes from being born again (Romans 5:1). This peace is not the absence of chaos, but it is the presence of tranquility while in the midst of chaos. Peace is a complete sense of knowing God controls the events of the day and not yourself (Philippians 4:6-7). Only God can give you the feeling of peace through the indwelling power of the Holy Spirit. God's peace is the freedom that He has given you to continue a "mess free" relationship with Him and to be able to rest while everything around you may be in turmoil (Galatians 5:1-26). A lot of this world's issues are the direct result of individual relationships, circumstances, and situations getting out of control because the parties involved refuse to seek God for His peace and understanding. You must be able to get to a place where you are at peace with whatever God sends your way and whatever God allows to happen in your life daily.

Ask Yourself...

(Before you complete the daily "Ask Yourself" questions, read the paragraph above and use your journal to record your answers and/or reflect throughout the day.)

Day 86: What are some of the things I do to live in peace with the people I interact with every day, such as my family, friends, and coworkers? Read Hebrews 12:14.

Day 87: Do I allow myself to become agitated, irritated, and mean when turmoil enters my life, or am I allowing the peace of God, which transcends all understanding, to guard my heart and my mind in Christ Jesus? Explain. Read Philippians 4:6.

Day 88: How have the daily evils in the world affected the peace in my life? Explain.

Day 89: If someone asked my closest friends and family members if I am a peaceful person, what would be their answer? Explain.

Day 90: Am I experiencing a life of peace on a regular basis, or do I allow my mind to go to the place where peace is nonexistent? Explain.

Day 91: Everyone has periods in their life when they are at peace. When I experience these moments, how does it feel to know that God is in control and is able to calm my inner stressors?

Day 92: In a perfect world, what would it look like to have "Peace on earth and good will towards men?" Read Luke 2:14.

Reflection Notes

_____

_____

_____

MEASURABLE OUTCOMES FOR LEVEL 1

Individual Mind

Day 93: Have you sacrificed at least 15 minutes a day for daily devotion and study on love, joy, and peace? This can consist of reading God's Word, meditation, seeking personal application, prayer, and implementing more love, joy, and peace in your daily interactions with everyone. If not, spend some time today to figure out how to increase your levels of these qualities.

Day 94: In what specific examples did your attitude towards love, joy, and peace change?

Day 95: Share what you learned about love, joy, or peace with someone you know may be struggling with any of these *Fruit of the Spirit* mentioned above.

Day 96: Now that you have done some reflection on love, joy, and peace, how have you handled situations that could have compromised your new-found knowledge of the topics?

Day 97: How is your journaling/self-reflection process going for the "Ask Yourself" questions in the activity?

Day 98: Were you able to start a Christian blog or social media presence sharing your journey in Level 1 of the Individual Mind section? Did you try to connect with others on a similar journey of discovery? If not, spend some time today to begin some chatter on Level 1 of the Mind section on some type of social media platform or in a face-to-face discussion with someone.

Day 99: What growth have you seen in your life as it pertains to the topics covered in Level 1 of the Mind section?

Day 100: What are some of the specific changes that you have noticed in your life since beginning Level 1 of the Mind section?

Reflection Notes

_____

_____

_____

_____

LEVEL 2

(PATIENCE, KINDNESS, AND GOODNESS)

PATIENCE

We have all heard the statement that "patience is a virtue," but what does that statement really mean? The first step to understanding its meaning is defining "patience," which is simply your ability to wait and not complain. If you want to connect that definition spiritually, having patience in Christ is your ability to endure moments of discomfort in your life without complaining or cursing God, as Job's wife instructed him to do (Job 2:9). If you are able to endure life's lows, valleys, trials, and tribulations at the hands of others (or your own) and not lash out and make situations worse, then patience is an actual virtue (Hebrews 10:35-38).

Your patience must try to mirror that of Jesus Christ, who was extremely patient with the men that supported and followed Him. At times, the disciples' laziness, arrogance, lack of discipline, and lack of belief in the power of Jesus could have easily forced Him to give up on them and find others to carry out His will. Even though Jesus was clearly frustrated at times with the disciples and He made statements to them that challenged their faith, He was patient with them. He was patient with Thomas, who still doubted who He was after Jesus defeated death and rose from the grave (John 20:24-29). Jesus displayed His level of humility, generosity, and patience by refusing to complain and show irritation in His daily interactions with them. You must continually humble yourself, as Jesus did, and not exercise your right to say justifiable statements to others in the moments you lack patience. This is a form of showing mercy on others. When you start to utilize the same patience that Jesus displayed, it shows your true commitment to Him and your continued anticipation of His glorious return.

Ask Yourself...

(Before you complete the daily "Ask Yourself" questions, read the paragraphs above and use your journal to record your answers and/or reflect throughout the day.)

Day 101: Do I believe that God is still in control even if He doesn't show up when I want or how I want Him to show up? Explain. Read Psalm 37:7. Am I okay with the way that God chooses to intercede in my life?

Day 102: What are my thoughts on the statement, "Good things come to those who wait"? Explain.

Day 103: What are my struggles with waiting calmly in normal life situations, such as waiting in line at the store or being stuck in traffic? Elaborate.

Day 104: How am I able to keep a godly perspective when things are extremely difficult in my life and it seems as if the difficulties are not ending any time soon? Explain.

Day 105: What things in my life have I been able to endure patiently? Elaborate.

Day 106: What things in my life have I not been able to endure patiently, and I wished I could get a "do over"? Elaborate.

Day 107: What will it take for me to have a godly perspective on life when things seem to be stuck in a revolving door or not progressing at all?

Reflection Notes

_____
_____
_____
_____
_____
_____
_____
_____
_____
_____

KINDNESS

Kindness is a very familiar term usually associated with some type of action that accompanies it. In order to get to the spiritual meaning of the word "kindness," we must look at how kindness is defined in the Greek language. "Kindness" in Greek is simply defined as "genuine concern." Kindness is one of the characteristics God displayed when He gave you salvation (Titus 3:4-5). Kindness played a major role in David's famous prayer in Psalm 23. It is the kindness of God that leads Him to do the things He does within that prayer. The genuine concern that God has for us is shown all throughout the Bible in His healings, His raising people from the dead, and His ability to continue to provide for those that didn't deserve it.

God's kindness then filters down to similar acts that Jesus displayed during His ministry. Kindness looks for ways to adapt to meet the needs of others in spite of your view or feelings about them. Kindness is also a moral goodness that overflows continuously with the help of God (Ephesians 4:31-32). As a Christian, you are to show the kindness that God has gifted you through your daily actions. Showing kindness means being able to put aside the differences, attitudes, and prejudices of those you come in contact with every day. The ability to show the kindness of God to those who make it clear that they don't like you, or may have even wronged you, must come from God (2 Corinthians 6:4-6). Remember that the same genuine concern God showed you, eventually leading to your salvation, must be present in your life so you can continue *Building a Victorious Christlike Life!*

Ask Yourself...

(Before you complete the daily "Ask Yourself" questions, read the paragraphs above and use your journal to record your answers and/or reflect throughout the day.)

Day 108: Do I believe that being kind is a trait that all Christians should have? Why? Read Colossians 3:12.

Day 109: Would other people say that I am a kind person? Explain why or why not.

Day 110: What are some of the remarkably kind things that I have done in the past few months? If I can't recall anything, I will try to show a remarkable act of kindness and record it today.

Day 111: Do I feel I have to be kind to everyone, including those who have hurt me? Explain.

Day 112: Do I serve others with kindness or am I too focused on my own needs, desires, or problems to let the goodness of God overflow to others? Explain.

Day 113: In what ways has God revealed His kindness in my life?

Day 114: What was the last act of remarkable kindness that someone, other than God, showed towards me? If I can't think of one, how has this affected me in being remarkably kind to other people?

Reflection Notes

_____
_____
_____
_____
_____
_____
_____
_____
_____

GOODNESS

"Good" can be defined in many ways because it plays out differently in the minds of all people. The safest way to define the word "good" or "goodness" is to use what God views as good. In Psalm 33:4-5, it speaks to the fact that this earth is full of the Lord's goodness. God has always intended for you to use His examples of goodness as your own. Our society has diluted God's meaning of good. You must decide what is wrong or right based on what God teaches you and not the fleshly view that is being used so frequently today. The goodness that God wants you to demonstrate daily is to show others your full commitment to right over wrong and good over evil. You must show a commitment to be led by God and not guided by Satan. Goodness reflects the character of God. The goodness in you should desire to see the goodness in others. Always remember that God is good all the time and all the time God is good. He wants you to continually grow and be transformed by the fruit of His goodness, ultimately striving to be as good to others as He has been to you!

Ask Yourself...

(Before you complete the daily "Ask Yourself" questions, read the paragraph above and use your journal to record your answers and/or reflect throughout the day.)

Day 115: How often do I feel the goodness of God flowing through my daily life? Explain. Read Exodus 33:19.

Day 116: How do I feel about the popular Christian saying, "God is good all the time and all the time God is good"? Explain.

Day 117: Do I reflect the goodness of God in my life so others will want to seek that same goodness in their life? If yes, explain how.

Day 118: How often do I desire to see goodness in others so they may experience God at a deeper level in their own lives? Explain.

Day 119: Even when life is tough, how does the goodness of God radiate through me? Explain.

Day 120: In what ways have I been good to others just as God has been good to me?

Day 121: When was the last time someone, other than God, showed goodness towards me? If I can't think of an example, has this affected me in being good to others?

Reflection Notes

MEASURABLE OUTCOMES FOR LEVEL 2

Individual Mind

Day 122: Have you sacrificed at least 15 minutes a day for devotion and study on patience, kindness, and goodness? This can consist of reading God's Word, meditating, seeking personal application, praying, and implementing more patience, kindness, and goodness in your daily interactions with everyone. If not, spend some time today to determine how to increase your levels of patience, kindness, and goodness.

Day 123: In what specific examples did your attitude towards patience, kindness, and goodness change?

Day 124: Share what you learned about patience, kindness, and goodness with someone that you know may be struggling with these Fruit of the Spirit.

Day 125: Now that you have done some reflection on patience, kindness, and goodness, how have you handled situations that could have compromised your new-found knowledge of these topics?

Day 126: How is your journaling/self-reflection process going on the "Ask Yourself" questions? Explain.

Day 127: Were you able to start a Christian blog or social media presence to share your journey in Level 2 of the Individual Mind section? Did you try to connect with others who are on a similar journey of discovery? If not, spend some time today to begin some chatter about Level 2 of the Mind section on some type of social media platform or in a face-to-face discussion with someone.

Day 128: What growth have you seen in your life as it pertains to the topics covered in Level 2 of the Mind section?

Day 129: What are some of the specific changes that you have noticed in your life since beginning Level 2 of the Mind section?

*All activities should include prayer and journaling for reflection purposes.

Reflection Notes

_____

_____

_____

LEVEL 3

(FAITHFULNESS, GENTLENESS, AND SELF-CONTROL)

FAITHFULNESS

Faithfulness is a *Fruit of the Spirit* that is on a steady decline as Satan continues to get in the mind of the believer and wreak havoc. Your faithfulness towards God and others starts in your mind, which is why you must keep your mind on God as much as possible. Being faithful has decreased as an important trait of a good character. Sin causes your faithfulness in relationships to decline. People are no longer faithful to their employers, and employers are no longer faithful to their employees. People are not only unfaithful to their spouses, but are even vocal about their unfaithfulness. In the past, this was at least frowned upon. People are also unfaithful to their children by neglecting their responsibility to raise them. Another example of unfaithfulness is when you fail to keep your word to God and to other people. Faith is your assurance that what God says in His Word is true (Hebrews 11:1).

Your faithfulness in all aspects of life, especially your faithfulness to God, is a direct reflection of how you allow the Holy Spirit to transform your life. The Holy Spirit stands as your seal of faithfulness that was gifted to you as a believer. The Holy Spirit living inside of you is your proof that God will remain faithful to you at all times, and you must take on that same approach and apply it to your relationships with both God and man. Without faith, you can't look past the evils of this world and see it getting better in the future (Hebrews 11:6). You must have the same faith in God that Noah and his family displayed. Noah's faith allowed him to trust the coming judgment of God in the form of rain flooding the earth. Even though rain didn't exist before the flood, Noah trusted the voice of God. He had a relationship with God, which led to his faithfulness to God. Noah's faithfulness led to his entire family being saved from God's judgment (Genesis 6:1–9:28). It takes faith for us to ignore the guiding of our sinful mind and be led by the Holy Spirit. Your faith helps you move closer to *Building a Victorious Christlike Life!*

Ask Yourself...

(Before you complete the daily "Ask Yourself" questions, read the paragraphs above and use your journal to record your answers and/or reflect throughout the day.)

Day 130: How has God been faithful to me? Explain. Read Psalm 26:3.

Day 131: How have I relied on God's faithfulness in my life to see me through difficult situations? Explain.

Day 132: In what ways is my life characterized by my faith in Christ? Explain.

Day 133: In what ways have I not been faithful to God? How has my lack of being faithful to God and His Word hurt others around me?

Day 134: In what ways can I increase my overall faith in God?

Day 135: In what ways can I lead those around me to increase their overall faith in God?

Day 136: How has a little bit of faith, like a mustard, seed accomplished God's will in my life? Read Matthew 2:20.

Reflection Notes

_____
_____
_____
_____
_____
_____
_____
_____
_____
_____
_____
_____
_____
_____
_____

GENTLENESS

When the Holy Spirit is working in you, leading to your spiritual transformation, one of the great traits that you inherit from God is gentleness. People often confuse gentleness with weakness, but gentleness is not absence of power or weakness (Matthew 11:28-30). Gentleness is more closely related to meekness. Being gentle revolves around humility to God and purposeful restraint in times of irritation or anger toward other people. Jesus was an extremely strong individual, and it takes a strong individual to display gentleness in his or her personal daily interactions.

You have this *Fruit of the Spirit* because God is asking you to allow Him to take control of your life and submit to His guidance by the Holy Spirit. Every individual is powerful in their own way, shape, or form, but utilizing God's gentleness in your life makes you a sharp tool while helping to build the Kingdom of God. When the Holy Spirit works in you and allows you to show gentleness, it gives you the ability to hold your tongue, quiet inappropriate opinions, and avoid inappropriate actions, which is power under control. Being gentle will lead you to become capable of recognizing that the ways of God are far more effective than your own (Isaiah 55:9). The transformed believer has a clear advantage over non-believers because the Holy Spirit even helps our gentleness with God when things don't go as planned. This leads to helping with your gentleness towards those you come into contact with daily. It is easier to attract flies with honey, which is sweet, than with vinegar, which is sour. When you are gentle with others, you attract them to Christ. The gift of gentleness allows you to be sweet and not sour when it comes to building God's Kingdom!

Ask Yourself...

(Before you complete the daily "Ask Yourself" questions, read the paragraph above and use your journal to record your answers and/or reflect throughout the day.)

Day 137: Do others view me as being gentle? Explain. Read Philippians 4:5.

Day 138: What are some of the benefits of being gentle when it comes to the relationships in my life?

Day 139: Do I come across to others as brash and headstrong, or am I allowing the gentleness of God to flow through me to others? Explain.

Day 140: What are some situations/interactions that I have had that I could have handled better by being gentler? Elaborate.

Day 141: How do I feel when people are not gentle to me? Explain.

Day 142: In what ways can I lead those around me to be gentler and use humility in our interactions?

Day 143: In what ways does being gentle with those around me lead to being able to forgive quickly? Read Matthew 18:23-25.

Reflection Notes

SELF-CONTROL

Self-control is a *Fruit of the Spirit* that is easy to define but, at times, difficult to implement. Self-control, also known as temperance, is choosing to be controlled by the Holy Spirit and not your fleshly desires (Romans 7:18-25). A clear sign that you are maturing when it comes to spiritual transformation is that you are allowing the Holy Spirit take over what you think, what you say, and what you do. Not allowing the Holy Spirit to lead and guide your daily interactions is not always a sign of a person that is weak. At times, it is a sign that you are allowing your sinful nature to show itself more than the Holy Spirit at that particular moment. Everyone knows that the light of God will always prevail over the darkness of this world, but at times there are moments of weakness. Without the power of the Holy Spirit it is impossible to fight your sinful nature, which leads you to a hopeless situation. The willing and sacrificial death of Jesus Christ freed you from the bondage and the penalty of sin (Galatians 5:1).

To better understand being free from the bondage of sin, consider that when you give your life to Christ, your old ways and thinking were crucified like Jesus was. Since your old self dies, this gives you the power to no longer be a slave to sin and wrong doing (Romans 6:6). Even though the Holy Spirit gifted you with self-control, if you allow Satan to turn your mind into his playground, then you are susceptible to bad decision-making in moments of weakness. A big part of accepting the responsibility of self-control as a Christian is valuing the big picture and not temporary satisfaction. God gave you the gift of self-control so you can protect your new self from your old self, leading to the transformed victorious Christlike life! One of the greatest benefits of self-control is being able to live a guilt-free life, which allows God to better utilize you for Kingdom building.

Ask Yourself...

(Before you complete the daily "Ask Yourself" questions, read the paragraphs above and use your journal to record your answers and/or reflect throughout the day.)

Day 144: In what areas/situations do I lack self-control? Explain. Read Proverbs 16:32.

Day 145: What are some of the consequences that I have had to endure because of my lack of self-control?

Day 146: Am I allowing fleshly desires or the Holy Spirit to control my life, leading me to a path of righteousness or a path of destruction? Explain.

Day 147: In what ways has my lack of proper self-control hurt me and my loved ones? Explain.

Day 148: What are five benefits to controlling my sinful desires? What are the benefits, if any, of not controlling my sinful desires?

Day 149: How does God bring glory to those who make valid attempts to properly practice self-control? Explain.

Day 150: How has having self-control been a blessing to those that are close to me?

Reflection Notes

_____
_____
_____
_____
_____
_____
_____
_____
_____
_____
_____
_____
_____
_____
_____
_____
_____
_____
_____
_____

MEASURABLE OUTCOMES FOR LEVEL 3

Individual Mind

Day 151: Have you sacrificed at least 15 minutes a day for daily devotion and study on faithfulness, gentleness, and self-control? This can consist of reading God's Word, meditating, seeking personal application, praying, and implementing more faithfulness, gentleness, and self-control in your daily interactions with everyone. If not, spend some time today to determine out how to increase your levels of faithfulness, gentleness, and self-control.

Day 152: In what specific examples did your attitude towards faithfulness, gentleness, and self-control change?

Day 153: Share what you learned about faithfulness, gentleness, and self-control with someone who you know may be struggling with the Fruit of the Spirit.

Day 154: Now that you have done some reflection on faithfulness, gentleness, and self-control, how have you handled situations that could have compromised your new-found knowledge?

Day 155: How is your journaling/self-reflection process going on the "Ask Yourself" questions in the activity?

Day 156: Were you able to start a Christian blog or social media presence sharing your journey through Level 3 of the Individual Mind section. Did you try to connect with others on a similar journey of discovery? If not, spend some time today to begin some chatter on Level 3 of the Mind section on some type of social media platform or in a face-to-face discussion with someone.

Day 157: What growth have you seen in your life as it pertains to the topics covered in Level 3 of this section on the Mind?

Day 158: What are some of the specific changes in your life that you have noticed since beginning Level 3 of the Mind section began?

Day 159: What overall changes have you noticed after completing the Mind portion of the Individual section of this interactive program? How was it beneficial?

*All activities should include prayer and journaling for reflection purposes.

Reflection Notes

Section Three

THE INDIVIDUAL

(THE BODY)

TAKING CARE OF YOUR BODY

(PLEASE CONSULT YOUR PHYSICIAN BEFORE IMPLEMENTING A NUTRITION

OR FITNESS PROGRAM OF ANY KIND.)

INSTRUCTIONS

You are about to embark on the last part of the awesome program, experiencing three different levels of the importance of the need for taking care of your earthly vessel, also known as your body. This process will highlight the importance that nutrition, exercise, and sleep/rest plays in the life of the believer. Once again, **PLEASE CONSULT YOUR PHYSICIAN BEFORE IMPLEMENTING A NUTRITION OR FITNESS PROGRAM OF ANY KIND.** This portion of the journey is meant to help guide you to live a more healthy and victorious life. By following this guide for your body, you will receive other benefits of both looking and feeling good, which also play a role in your daily attitudes and outlook on life.

This guide is set up to have you focus on one question/bullet point per day, which in turn can be used as your daily spiritual devotion. It will consist of at least **15 minutes** of self-reflection, Scripture reading, prayer, meditation, and worship, eventually leading to your overall growth as a Christian. The first level of the Individual Body section will consist of exploring proper nutrition. The second level of the Body section will consist of examining proper exercise and fitness. The third level of the Body section will consist of reviewing proper sleep and rest. Before beginning this interactive program, log your starting weight and waist measurements. Also, research any sickness that you may be suffering from (high blood pressure, for example) and take note of your clothing sizes. If possible, purchase a smart watch, a fitness tracker, or download a fitness app to help monitor your daily activity and progress.

INTRODUCTION

The popular saying goes like this: "Take care of your body, and it will take care of you." As a Christian, your body is God's temple. He only gave you one body, and it is your responsibility to respectfully care for it. Once you have accepted Jesus as your Lord and Savior, God gives you His Holy Spirit to live inside of you. The Holy Spirit then helps you live up to God's holy expectation. God purchased you with the priceless death of His one-of-a-kind Son, Jesus Christ. Since the price was so high, you should feel obligated to care for the holy temple that God gave you (1 Corinthians 6:19-20). It is vital that you take care of your soul, mind, and even your body so you can be healthy and do the work that He has called you to do (3 John 2).

Your body, God's temple, is fearfully and wonderfully made(Psalm 139:14); and you were put in charge to care for it. Developing a wellness-based lifestyle (based on the principles of healthy nutrition, exercise, sleep, and rest) can assist you (along with your family and community) in becoming a better steward of God's temple (1 Corinthians 6:19).

LEVEL 1

NUTRITION

(PLEASE CONSULT YOUR PHYSICIAN BEFORE IMPLEMENTING A NUTRITION OR FITNESS PROGRAM OF ANY KIND.)

TAKING CONTROL OF WHAT YOU PUT INTO YOUR BODY

Just as you need to be mindful of what you put into your body mentally and spiritually, you must also be mindful of the quality and quantity of the food and drinks that you consume daily. Even though there are plenty of ways to consume your daily intake of calories, it is recommended that you eat at least three healthy meals per day (preferably home cooked or healthy choices from outside sources). You also should consume three to seven servings of fruits and vegetables per day. (A serving size is equivalent to the size of your fist.)

Breakfast

On a daily basis, eat a healthy breakfast with fruit and/or raw nuts before or after morning prayer and Scripture reading (John 21:12; Matthew 6:33). A healthy breakfast can also include steel-cut oatmeal, low-sugar cereals, turkey bacon, whole-wheat toast, and other nutritious breakfast items. **If you have a nut allergy, SUBSTITUTE unsalted seeds without shells.**

Lunch

A healthy lunch can include lean meats such as turkey, chicken, and fish. Cooked meats should be baked, grilled, or broiled. Lunch can also include a salad (with spinach, tomatoes, etc.) or sandwich (with whole-wheat or multi-grain bread, spinach, tomatoes, turkey, chicken, etc.). Use dressings and other condiments sparingly.

Dinner

A healthy dinner can include chicken, turkey, fish (baked, grilled, or broiled), two servings of vegetables (broccoli, spinach, cauliflower, etc.), brown rice, quinoa, black beans, and/or other healthy food items.

Snacks

Healthy snacks can include grapes, strawberries, apples, watermelon, almonds, pistachios, and similar fruits and/or raw nuts or seeds. Healthy snacks should be consumed between meals and well-planned. **If you have a nut allergy, SUBSTITUTE unsalted seeds without shells.**

Liquids (Drinks)

Consume seven 8-ounce glasses of WATER per day. REPLACE soda, diet soda, energy drinks, and other sugary drinks with water.

Ask Yourself...

(Before you complete the daily "Ask Yourself" questions, read the paragraph above and use your journal to record your answers and/or reflect throughout the day.)

Day 160: Do I believe that since God gave me life and my body, it is my responsibility to respect it by what I do to it and by what I put in it? Explain.

Day 161: How many square meals do I eat daily and is any of the food that I eat healthy? Explain.

Day 162: What is keeping me from eating properly? Elaborate.

Day 163: What are the benefits of eating properly?

Day 164: How does having a healthier body affect my relationship with God?

Day 165: Do I feel that the self-control shown by how I eat is a direct reflection of my level of spiritual self-control and how it plays out? Explain.

Day 166: Do I know anyone who has been hindered in doing what God called them to do because of their refusal to eat properly? Explain.

Reflection Notes

MEASURABLE OUTCOMES FOR LEVEL 1

Individual Body

Day 167: Do you feel that committing to starting every morning with a balanced breakfast and morning devotion, including revisiting some of the lessons from the Individual Soul and the Individual Mind sections, would be beneficial? How soon will you begin to implement these practices?

Day 168: What benefits do you feel you will receive by adding a few minutes of prayer and a devotional reading of your choice every day with your breakfast?*

Day 169: Have you seen any changes in how you feel even in this past week? Make a note of your current body weight, measurements, and eating habits and try to track your progress both positive and negative.

Day 170: Reflect and record in your journal what you ate yesterday. Did it fit within this new guide? (Write down everything you consumed the day before.)

Day 171: Have you told someone about the new eating guide so they can hold you accountable when you are tempted by some of your former choices? If yes, how did it go? If not, implement this today.

Day 172: Have you talked about your progress and new guide on social media to encourage others and so that they can inquire about what you are doing? If not, what is keeping you from doing this?

Day 173: What benefits have you seen in your life as it pertains to your nutrition?

Day 174: What are some of the specific changes have you noticed since beginning this nutrition guide?

*All activities should include prayer and journaling for reflection purposes.

Reflection Notes

_____

_____

_____

_____

LEVEL 2

PHYSICAL ACTIVITY

(PLEASE CONSULT YOUR PHYSICIAN BEFORE IMPLEMENTING A NUTRITION OR FITNESS PROGRAM OF ANY KIND.)

TAKING CONTROL OF WHAT YOU DO TO YOUR BODY

Even as Christians, working out and being fit is a direct reflection of how much you care about the temple that God has blessed you to use while on earth. Working out is also connected to gaining more discipline in our everyday living. The Bible is clear that we should take good care of our bodies (1 Corinthians 6:19-20). The Bible also teaches against vanity. Looking good is one of the many benefits of exercising, but we can't let it go to our heads and become our main focus (1 Samuel 16:7; Proverbs 32:30; 1 Peter 3:3-4). It is imperative to find the balance in order to get all of the other benefits of exercising. Your goal of exercising should NOT be for the admiration of others; it should be for your overall goal of improved physical health. This will lead you to be able to carry out God's Vision for your life in the way He sees fit. Another benefit of exercising is the production of more energy. This energy can be used to help yourself, others around you, and the Kingdom of God.

Exercising

You should exercise at least three days per week, preferably every other day if possible. Each workout should last 30 minutes and include the following:

◊ 10 minutes of interval (slow, fast, slow, fast, etc.) cardio—Cardio can include running, jumping rope, etc.

◊ 10 minutes of circuit training—These are the type of exercises that work the upper and lower body. For example, they can be burpees followed by body weight squats with a 30-second rest between each set. (Refer to the internet for an example of what a burpee looks like.)

◊ 10 minutes of interval cardio—Cardio can include stair climbing, bike riding, etc.

Leisurely Active Days

On your non-workout days (i.e., the other four days of the week), be leisurely active by participating in physical fitness activities such as swimming, walking, tennis, basketball, etc.

- ◊ Try walking after a meal and get in tune with God and nature.

- ◊ Choose something fun and it won't feel like you are working out.

Ask Yourself...

(Before you complete the daily "Ask Yourself" questions, read the paragraph above and use your journal to record your answers and/or reflect throughout the day.)

Day 175: What are some of the benefits of exercising? (Do a little research.)

Day 176: How does taking care of my body through exercising help with Kingdom building?

Day 177: How many times a week do I currently do at least 30 minutes of physical activity, and what are those activities?

Day 178: What ways can I rearrange my life to ensure I am getting the physical activity needed to create more energy and take care of my body?

Day 179: What types of activities can I see my self doing on my leisure days to ensure I am getting a fun break but still moving around?

Day 180: Do I feel that the self-control of exercising is a direct reflection of my spiritual self-control? Explain.

Day 181: Do I know anyone who has been hindered in doing what God has called them to do because of their refusal to exercise? Explain.

Reflection Notes

_____
_____
_____
_____

MEASURABLE OUTCOMES FOR LEVEL 2

Individual Body

Day 182: Do you feel that starting your day with 15 minutes of devotion with God gives you the strength and energy to exercise and become healthier for His use while reflecting on some of the lessons from the Individual sections on the Soul and the Mind? How soon will you begin to implement this?

Day 183: What benefits do you receive by taking the time to plan out your exercise and leisure days for the week?

Day 184: Have you had an opportunity to purchase a smart watch to help with monitoring your fitness and overall health goals? When your goals are tangible, you are better able to reach them.

Day 185: Get a workout buddy, if you don't have one, to hold you accountable and to make sure you are adhering to your workout days.

Day 186: Commit to reading some books or journals on health, and try to seek some different types of workouts and routines to keep it fresh.

Day 187: Do you feel that sharing your progress is beneficial to others? If yes, post your progress on social media so others can see that you are taking your body back with the hope that they will be inspired to do so also.

Day 188: What benefits have you seen in your life as it pertains to your fitness and exercise?

Day 189: What are some of the specific changes you have noticed since your fitness and exercise routine has changed?

*All activities should include prayer and journaling for reflection purposes.

LEVEL 3

SLEEP/REST

TAKING CONTROL OF YOUR RECOVERY TIME

Sleep plays a vital role in your overall physical health. Sleep allows your body to continue to heal and to repair your heart and blood vessels after a long day. Lack of sleep is directly connected to multiple serious diseases, such as an increased risk of heart disease, kidney disease, high blood pressure, diabetes, and stroke. It is extremely difficult to take care of your loved ones and give them what they need if you haven't recovered from the previous day. Even though your body is "fearfully and wonderfully made," it can only take so much without proper sleep, rest, and moments of relaxation.

Sleep

High quality sleep is one of the best things we can do for our health. Following evening prayer and Scripture reading, we should get at least an uninterrupted seven hours of sleep if it is within our control (see Psalm 4:8).

- ◊ Keep the bedroom dark.

- ◊ Keep the bedroom cool.

Rest

Make sure you input at least one rest day during your busy week to prevent yourself from burning out. Mental fatigue is just as bad as physical fatigue; without giving your mind some time to rest and recharge, you CANNOT function properly. You must make the mental adjustment to understand the need for and enforce mental days off so you can better serve those in your immediate circle (see Genesis 2:3; Deuteronomy 5:12-15; Mark 2:27; 6:31).

- ◊ Try to build in a day of rest and relaxation to get a break from the everyday hustle.

- If you can't build in a day of rest, set aside a half of day.

- If you can't build in a half of day, try to schedule a few hours here and there to relax your mind.

- If you can't find a few hours here and there, then you need to rearrange your life before your rest is forced in a hospital bed!

Ask Yourself...

(Before you complete the daily "Ask Yourself" questions, read the paragraph above and use your journal to record your answers and/or reflect throughout the day.)

Day 190: About how many hours of sleep per night do I receive? Try getting a smart watch to track the length and quality of your sleep.

Day 191: Is my life set up to be able to get high quality sleep and moments of rest? Explain.

Day 192: Are things like stress, work, kids, and unhappiness keeping me from good sleep and rest? Explain.

Day 193: Do I understand the importance and benefits of both sleep and rest? Does my daily schedule have time for God? Explain.

Day 194: What do I need to do to ensure that my body is getting proper recovery day-in and day-out?

Day 195: Do I feel that being unable to get proper rest is a direct reflection of potential stressors that need to be addressed? Elaborate.

Day 196: Do I know anyone who has been hindered in doing what God has called them to do because they do not give their body proper rest and relaxation time? Explain.

Reflection Notes

MEASURABLE OUTCOMES FOR LEVEL 3

Individual Body

Day 197: Start your day with 15 minutes of devotion through prayer and meditation. You should be well rested from the previous night so this should be easy.*

Day 198: How beneficial would it be to start your morning devotion by revisiting some of the lessons from the Individual Soul and the Individual Mind sections? Have you started this process?

Day 199: During a moment of rest, journal about how good God has been to you and what you feel you can work on in order to be put to better use by God.

Day 200: Try to free up enough time to get involved in some type of ministry at your church.

Day 201: Set your rest goals at the start of each week and make sure you are following the schedule that you have developed. Give yourself a moment of rest to do something that you enjoy that God wouldn't mind you doing (for example, a fun activity the enables you to laugh and live momentarily stress free).

Day 202: What benefits have you seen in your life as it pertains to your recovery, sleep, and rest?

Day 203: What are some of the specific changes you have noticed since guarding your recovery, sleep, and rest?

Day 204: What overall changes have you noticed after completing the Individual Body section of this interactive activity? Was it beneficial?

Day 205: Now that you have completed this version of the book, what are your overall thoughts about what you have experienced? Did your total experience with this program lead to a better understanding of why transforming your soul, mind, and body are so important when Building Victorious Christlike Lives?

*All activities should include prayer and journaling for reflection purposes.

Reflection Notes

About the Publisher

LIFE TO LEGACY LLC

Let us bring your story to life! Life to Legacy offers the following publishing services: manuscript development, editing, transcription services, ghost writing, cover design, copyright services, ISBN assignment, worldwide distribution, and eBooks.

Throughout the entire production process, you maintain control over your project. Even if you have no manuscript, we can ghost-write your story for you from audio recordings or legible handwritten documents. Whether print-on-demand or trade publishing, we have publishing packages to meet your needs. We make the production and publishing processes easy for you.

We also specialize in family history books, so you can leave a written legacy for your children, grandchildren, and others. You put your story in our hands, and we'll bring it to literary life!

Please visit our website:
www.Life2Legacy.com

Or call us at:
877-267-7477

You can also e-mail us at:
Life2Legacybooks@att.net

www.ingramcontent.com/pod-product-compliance
Lightning Source LLC
Chambersburg PA
CBHW080448110426
42743CB00016B/3318